HOW TO
SIT

THICH NHAT HANH

PARALLAX PRESS

BERKELEY, CALIFORNIA

Parallax Press
P.O. Box 7355
Berkeley, California 94710

Parallax Press is the publishing division of Plum
Village Community of Engaged Buddhism, Inc.
Copyright © 2014 Plum Village Community
of Engaged Buddhism, Inc.
Printed in The United States of America

Cover and text design by Debbie Berne
Illustrations by Jason DeAntonis
Edited by Rachel Neumann

ISBN: 978-1-937006-58-7

Library of Congress Cataloging-in-Publication Data
Nhat Hanh, Thich, author.
How to sit / Thich Nhat Hanh.
    pages cm
Includes bibliographical references.
ISBN 978-1-937006-58-7
1. Meditation—Buddhism. I. Title.
BQ5612.N474 2014
294.3'4435—dc23
                                          2014000019

7 8 / 20 19

CONTENTS

The first thing to do is to stop
whatever else you are doing.

Now sit down somewhere comfortable.

Anywhere is fine.

Notice your breathing.

As you breathe in,
be aware
that you are
breathing in.

As you breathe out,
notice that you are
breathing out.

NOTES ON SITTING

Many of us spend a lot of time sitting—too much time. We sit at our jobs, we sit at our computers, and we sit in our cars. To *sit*, in this book, means to sit in such a way that you enjoy sitting, to sit in a relaxed way, with your mind awake, calm, and clear. This is what we call *sitting*, and it takes some training and practice.

BODY, MIND, AND BREATH

In our daily lives, our attention is dispersed. Our body is in one place, our breath is ignored, and our mind is wandering. As soon as we pay attention to our breath, as we breathe in, these three things—body, breath, and mind—come together. This can happen in just one or two seconds. You come back to yourself. Your awareness brings these three elements together, and you become fully present in the here and the now. You are taking care of your body, you are taking care of your breath, and you are taking care of your mind.

When you make a soup, you have to add together all the right ingredients in harmony and let them simmer. Our breath is the broth that brings the different elements together. We bathe spirit and mind in our breath and they become integrated so they are one thing. We are whole.

We don't need to control our body, mind, and breath. We can just be there for them. We allow them to be themselves. This is nonviolence.

PEACE IS CONTAGIOUS

The energy of mindfulness can help improve your whole being. Just pay attention to your in-breath. Allow it to be the way it is and you will see that the quality of your breathing naturally becomes calmer, deeper, and more harmonious all by itself. This is the power of simple recognition. When your breath is deeper and more peaceful, it will have an influence right away on your body and your mind. Peace and calm are contagious.

A BOAT ON THE OCEAN

Imagine a boat full of people crossing the
ocean. The boat is caught in a storm. If anyone
panics and acts rashly they will endanger the
boat. But if there's even one person who is
calm, this person can inspire calm in others.
Such a person can save the whole boat. That's
the power of non-action. Our quality of being
is the ground of all appropriate action. When
we look closely at our actions and the actions
of those around us, we can see the quality of
being behind these actions.

DOING NOTHING

Imagine trees standing together in a forest. They don't talk, but they feel each other's presence. When you look at them, you might say they aren't doing anything. But they are growing and providing clean air for living things to breathe. Instead of describing sitting meditation as the practice of concentration, looking deeply, and getting insight, I like to describe sitting as enjoying doing nothing. Primarily, sitting is to enjoy the pleasure of sitting, being fully alive and in touch with the wonders of our working bodies, the cool air, the sounds of people and birds, and the changing colors of the sky.

MEDITATION

The term for sitting and being aware is sitting meditation. "Zen" is the Japanese pronunciation of *dhyana*, which is the Sanskrit word for meditation. Meditation is simply the practice of stopping and looking deeply. You do not need to sit to meditate. Anytime you are looking deeply—whether you are walking, chopping vegetables, brushing your teeth, or going to the bathroom—you can be meditating. In order to look deeply, you need to make the time to stop everything and see what is there.

With mindfulness and concentration you can direct your attention to what is there and have a deep look. You can begin to see the true nature of what is in front of you. What is there may be a cloud, a pebble, or a human being. It may be our anger. Or it may be our own body and its nature of impermanence. Every time we truly stop and look deeply, the result is a better understanding of the true nature of what is there inside us and around us.

DON'T JUST DO SOMETHING, SIT THERE

When people say, "Don't just sit there, do something," they're urging you to act. But if the quality of your being is poor—if you don't have enough peace, understanding, and equanimity, if you still have a lot of anger and worries—then your actions will also be poor. Your actions should be based on the foundation of a high quality of being. Being is non-action, so the quality of action depends on the quality of non-action. Non-action is already something. There are people who don't seem to do very much, but their presence is crucial for the well-being of the world. You may know people like this, who are steady, not always busy doing things, not making a lot of money, or being engaged in a lot of projects, but who are very important to you; the quality of their presence makes them truly available. They are contributing non-action, the high quality of their presence. To be in the here and the now—solid and fully alive—is a very positive contribution to our collective situation.

THE MONK ON THE PLATFORM

When I was a novice monk in Vietnam, I went to a temple called Hai Duc where I saw a Zen master sitting. He wasn't in the meditation hall. He was sitting on a simple platform made from perhaps five planks of wood. It was painted brown and was very clean. On the platform was a small table with four legs that were a little bit bent. That little table had a vase of flowers on it. I saw the Zen master sitting on the platform, facing the table. He was sitting very naturally and peacefully, his spine straight and his body at ease.

As a young child, I saw a drawing of the Buddha sitting on the grass. He looked very free, relaxed, and peaceful, as well as very kind. Now I was seeing a real human being sitting like that. This was a person like me, not an illustration or someone belonging to another world. Seeing the monk on the platform was a very holy experience. I wanted to be able to sit like that monk. I knew that sitting like that would bring me happiness.

DOING LESS

Many of us keep trying to do more and more. We do things because we think we need to, because we want to make money, accomplish something, take care of others, or make our lives and our world better. Often we do things without thinking, because we are in the habit of doing them, because someone asks us to, or because we think we should. But if the foundation of our being is not strong enough, then the more we do, the more troubled our society becomes.

Sometimes we do a lot, but we don't really do anything. There are many people who work a lot. There are people who seem to meditate a lot, spending many hours a day doing sitting meditation, chanting, reciting, lighting a lot of incense, but who never transform their anger, frustration, and jealousy. This is because the quality of our being is the basis of all our actions. With an attitude of accomplishing, judging, or grasping, all of our actions—even our meditation—will have that quality. The quality of our presence is the most positive element that we can contribute to the world.

ENJOY YOUR BREATHING

When you sit down, the first thing to do is to become aware of your breathing. Becoming aware of your breathing is the first step in taking care of yourself. Becoming aware of your in-breath and out-breath, you can see how your breath moves through your body. You begin to take care of your body and your mind, and you begin to find joy in the very simple act of breathing. Every in-breath can bring joy; every out-breath can bring calm and relaxation. This is a good enough reason to sit. We don't need to sit with an intention like getting smarter or becoming enlightened. We can sit just to enjoy sitting and breathing.

THE JOY OF MEDITATION

If you ask a child, "Why are you eating choco-late? The child would likely answer, "Because I like it." There's no purpose in eating the choc-olate. Suppose you climb a hill and stand on top to look around. You might feel quite happy standing on the hill. There's not a reason for doing it. Sit in order to sit. Stand in order to stand. There is no goal or aim in sitting. Do it because it makes you happy.

A CELEBRATION

If you are breathing mindfully in and out, you already have insight. Everyone is breathing, but not everyone is aware that they're breathing. When you breathe in mindfully, you realize that you are alive. If you weren't alive, you wouldn't be breathing in. To be alive is the greatest of all miracles, and you can rejoice in being alive. When you breathe in this way, your breath is a celebration of life.

FOLLOWING OUR BREATH

Mindfulness is always mindfulness of *something*. When we are mindful, we are paying attention, but what are we paying attention to? Mindfulness always has an object. When we sit, we can become aware of our in-breath and out-breath. Follow your breath from the beginning of each inhale all the way through the end of each exhale. This is mindfulness of breathing. Each time we practice mindful breathing, we know a little more what mindfulness feels like.

LOOKING DEEPLY

Sitting meditation is a practice that helps us heal and transform. It helps us to be whole, and to look deeply into ourselves and into what's around us in order to see clearly what is really there. Looking deeply, we light up the recesses of our mind and look into the heart of things in order to see their true nature.

MEDITATION IN DAILY LIFE

When most people hear the word "meditation,"
they think of sitting meditation. There are many
different kinds of meditation. Mindfulness
meditation can be practiced anywhere and
in whatever position the body is in—whether
we are sitting, walking, standing, or lying
down. Whenever we perform our daily activi-
ties with mindful awareness, we're practicing
meditation.

WISDOM

By looking deeply, the meditation practitioner
gains insight or wisdom, *prajña*. Insight has the
power to liberate us from our own suffering
and bondage. In the process of meditation,
fetters are undone; internal blocks of suffering such as resentment, fear, anger, despair,
and hatred are transformed; relationships
with humans and nature become easier; freedom and joy can penetrate us. We become
aware of what is inside and around us; we are
fresher and more alive in our daily lives. As we
become freer and happier, we cease to act in
ways that make others suffer, and we are able
to bring about change in ourselves and help
others around us become free.

WHY SIT?

When we sit, we bring joy and nourishment to
ourselves and to others. Every time we sit, we
can sit in such a way that the world can profit
from our sitting. We are solid. We are relaxed.
We are calm. We are happy while sitting. We
sit as if we are sitting on a lotus flower, not on
a heap of burning charcoal.

THE MOMENT OF ENLIGHTENMENT

Siddhartha, the man who became the Buddha many years ago in India, sat for a long time at the foot of the Bodhi tree. He appeared just to be sitting, but his body was also participating in his awakening. He was very closely observing his body, his feelings, and his perceptions. As he continued to practice, his power of mindfulness and concentration became stronger and stronger. One day at dawn, as the Morning Star appeared, he felt a liberation that dissipated all the darkness within him. That was the moment of enlightenment.

THE NON-PRACTICE PRACTICE

There are some people who sit in a very funny way; they try to show that they are practicing sitting meditation. When you breathe in mindfully and joyfully, don't try to show off to other people as if you were saying, "You know, I am breathing in mindfully." Don't worry what your sitting looks like from the outside. Practice the non-practice practice. We can best convey the essence of the practice to others simply by doing it with our whole being.

ARRIVING HOME

When you sit, sit in such a way that you feel
you have already arrived. To sit doesn't mean
to struggle. When you sit, sit so that sitting
becomes an arrival into the present moment.
Enjoy your arrival. How wonderful to have
arrived. How wonderful to feel that you are
home, that your true home is in the here
and the now. Sitting like that, joy and peace
become a reality. You radiate this joy and
peace and it benefits everyone around you.

FREEDOM

In the present moment, we can be free from regret concerning the past and from fear concerning the future. Happiness isn't possible without freedom. Coming back to the present moment, we are released from our worries, our fears, our regrets, our projects, and our busyness.

NOURISH YOURSELF
WHEREVER YOU ARE

It's wonderful if you have a quiet place to sit
at home or in your workplace. But you can
practice mindful sitting wherever you are. If
you ride the train or the bus to work, these are
excellent places to practice sitting. Instead of
thinking about your projects, your colleagues,
your list of tasks, you can enjoy practicing
breathing in and out to release the tension in
your body and give your mind a break from
being caught in thinking. You can create a
meditation hall of your bus or your train. Use
your time, wherever you are, to nourish and
heal yourself.

SITTING COMFORTABLY

When you sit, keep your spinal column quite straight, while allowing your body to be relaxed. When your sitting posture is relaxed and stable, you can sit comfortably for a long time. You embody solidity and this helps your mind to be calm. A stable posture grounds body and mind. Sitting still, we minimize the actions of body, speech, and mind so we're not pulled hither and thither by thoughts and feelings in which we might otherwise drown.

UNDER THE BODHI TREE

A gatha is a traditional short verse that you can recite during your meditation. You can make your own, or recite ones you have heard. Here is one:

Sitting here
is like sitting under the bodhi tree.
My body is mindfulness itself,
entirely free from distraction.

SITTING IN PRISON

A Vietnamese student of mine studied English literature at Indiana University before returning to Vietnam and being ordained as a nun. As a nun, she was very active in trying to ease the suffering of people's daily lives. She was arrested by the police and put into prison because of her actions. She would practice sitting meditation in her prison cell. It was difficult, because the guards saw her sitting as a provocative action. They thought she was defying them by sitting peacefully. She would wait until night, when all the lights were off, so she could sit like a free person. The people who put her in prison were trying to control her. She had to practice so she wouldn't lose her mind; sitting like that gave her space in her heart. She also taught others who were incarcerated how to sit and breathe so that they would suffer less. In her outer form, she was caught in prison. Yet she was completely free. If you can sit like that, the walls are not there. You are in touch with the whole universe. You have more freedom than people outside who are imprisoning themselves with their agitation and anger. People can try to steal many things from us, but they can't steal our determination and our practice.

EASE

Sit in such a way that you feel completely at ease. Relax every muscle in your body, including the muscles in your face. The best way to relax the muscles in your face is to smile gently as you breathe in and out. Don't make a great effort, or struggle, or fight as you sit. Let go of everything. This prevents backache, shoulderache, or headache. If you are able to find a cushion that fits your body well, you can sit for a long time without feeling tired.

WHAT TO DO

Sometimes people say they don't know what to do when they are sitting. "You only need to sit" is an exhortation of the Soto Zen meditation school. It means that you should sit without waiting for a miracle, and that includes the miracle of enlightenment. If you always sit in expectation, you're not in the present moment. The present moment contains the whole of life.

LETTING GO

Sit in such a way that you feel light, relaxed, happy, and free. Many of us have so many anxieties and projects that weigh heavily on us. We carry our past sorrows and anger and they become a kind of baggage that makes life heavy. Sitting meditation is a way to practice letting go of the things we carry needlessly. These things are nothing but obstacles to our happiness. Ease in our sitting and ease in our breathing nourishes the body and mind.

When we are calm, we can look deeply into a difficult emotion to see its roots and understand it better. First, we nourish ourselves with the joy of meditation, calming the breath, body, and thoughts. Then we embrace the difficult feeling. This brings some relief and gives us a more solid basis for investigating and transforming the difficulty so we can get the healing we need.

Finally, we can explore if our emotion is based on something happening in the present or something that we are still attached to from the past. If it's from the past we can begin to let it go, to more truly see and experience the present moment.

SMILING

As you sit, consider smiling lightly. This should be a natural smile, not a grimace or a forced smile. Your smile relaxes all your facial muscles. When you smile to your whole body, it is as if you are bathed in a fresh, cool stream of water.

HAPPINESS

Relaxing and calming the body as we breathe in and out, we can already experience joy and happiness. This is the joy of being alive, of being able to nourish the body at the same time as the soul. To sit knowing that we don't have to do anything but breathe in and out in awareness is a great happiness. Countless people bounce about like yo-yos in their busy lives and never have the chance to taste this joy. Don't worry if you don't have hours to dedicate to sitting. A few moments of sitting and conscious breathing can bring great happiness.

BREATHING ROOM

Every time you sit, whether it's at work, at the foot of a tree, or on your meditation cushion at home, enjoy your sitting. Then you won't consider sitting to be hard practice. It's very pleasant. Set aside a room or a corner or a cushion that you use just for sitting. When you arrive there, you will immediately begin to feel some of the joy and relaxation that comes from sitting. Whether sitting alone or with a few friends, you can produce your full presence, your true presence.

SITTING WITH THE BELL

The sound of the bell is a wonderful way to begin sitting meditation. The sound of the bell is the voice of your own true self, calling you back to the present moment. The beautiful sound reminds us that our true home is in the present moment. Listening to the bell supports meditation practice. Be aware of your breathing when listening to the bell.

INVITING THE BELL

Instead of "striking the bell," I like to say "inviting the bell to sound." Breathe in and out three times and then wake up the bell by touching the inviter to the bell and leaving it there, causing a muffled sound. Then breathe in and out one time before inviting a full sound of the bell. If you don't have a bell, you can download a recording of the sound of the bell onto your phone or computer.*

*http://plumvillage.org/mindfulness-practice/
mindfulness-software/

LISTENING TO THE BELL

When we sit and listen to the bell, we can allow all the cells in our body to listen to the sound. The mind is also made of something like "cells." These are our thoughts, feelings, and perceptions, and our ideas about how things are and should be. All the mental formations exist in the unconscious mind as seeds. When a seed, for example the seed of anger, is touched, it manifests in the conscious mind and there we call it a mental formation. Whatever mental formation has arisen in us, we can allow it to listen to the bell. Whether it is worry, anger, fear, or attachment, we allow the mental formation to listen to the bell with us. Just as a flower is made of non-flower elements, we are made of non-us elements. We are made of ancestors, culture, food, air, and water. We are made of form, feelings, perceptions, mental formations, and consciousness. We invite every component to listen deeply to the bell. This way of listening brings peace into every cell of the body and mind.

ACCOMPANYING YOUR BREATH

If you have a bell at home, anyone can invite it at any time to bring everyone back to themselves. Every time you hear the bell, you stop everything you are saying, doing, or thinking. Ride on the sound of the bell and on your breath to go home to yourself, to go home to the present moment, to the here and the now. You learn the art of being alive, of being present. To be alive means to be in the here and the now so we can be in touch with the wonders of life within us and around us. The practice is simple. Every time you hear the bell, it's as if someone is calling you, "Come home, my child, don't run anymore. Come home to yourself. Come home to life."

CREATING A GOOD HABIT

If you sit regularly, it will become a habit. You will let go of trying to arrive anywhere. Even the Buddha still practiced sitting every day after his enlightenment. There is nowhere to arrive except the present moment.

HABIT ENERGY

When you sit, you may feel something pushing you to get up and do something else. That's the energy inside each of us called habit energy. Habit energy is energy that is fueled by an old pattern, situation, or habit. It isn't based on our real needs and our real situation in the present.

Habit energy is always pushing. We have the habit of thinking that happiness isn't possible in the here and now, that we have to go and look for it somewhere else or in the future.

That's why we keep running. Our parents ran too. They transmitted the habit of running to us, and they received it from their ancestors. It's a longstanding habit. We deeply believe that in the future we may have more conditions for our happiness and that our "real life" lies somewhere else. It's because of our habit energy, that the present moment can seem boring.

It is a strong energy. If we are not aware of it, it can be stronger than we are. When we sit and invite the sound of the bell, it is a reminder to let go of that habit energy and return home.

ON THE BUS IN INDIA

Some years ago I went to India to give retreats
for the Dalit people. They're considered the
lowest caste in Indian society, and have been
discriminated against for thousands of years.
Many of them have embraced Buddhism
because there are no castes in Buddhist practice. A Dalit man from the Buddhist Society
was helping organize our tour. He had a family,
an apartment in New Delhi, and a comfortable
material life, but he still carried the habit energies of his class and the discrimination against
him. I was sitting next to him in the bus, enjoying looking out of the window at the landscape
of India. When I turned my head back, I saw
him sitting in a very tense way. While I was
enjoying sitting in the bus, he wasn't enjoying

it at all. I said, "Dear friend, I know that you're eager to make my visit pleasant and happy. I'm feeling very comfortable and happy right now, so please sit back and relax, don't worry." He said, "Okay," and he sat back and relaxed while I looked out of the window again and enjoyed the scenery. When I looked back a few minutes later, I saw him again as rigid as before, because those worries, feelings, and that tendency always to be struggling had been handed down to him by many generations of ancestors. It's not easy just to stop and recognize old habit energies. We all need a friend to help remind us from time to time. If no one else is there, the sound of the bell can be that friend, reminding us to recognize and smile at our old habit energies. In that way, we can become free of them.

SEEING CLEARLY

The first thing to do when you sit down is
to pay attention to your in-breath and out-
breath. Focus your attention entirely on your
breathing. If you truly practice, your breath
will become peaceful. This peaceful breathing will soothe both mind and body. This is
the first priority of sitting meditation, to help
us calm down. Once we are calm, we can see
more clearly. And when our vision is no longer
clouded, we see with more understanding,
and we naturally begin to feel compassion for
ourselves and for others. That is when true
happiness becomes possible.

GIFTS OF THE PRACTICE

Sitting and breathing mindfully brings four important elements into our lives: peace, clarity, compassion, and courage. When we are peaceful and clear, we are inspired to be more compassionate. Compassion brings courage, and courage brings true happiness. When you have great compassion in yourself, you have the capacity to act with courage. You have enough courage to look deeply at old habits, acknowledge fear, and make decisions that can cut through craving and anger. If you don't have enough compassion for yourself and for others, you won't have the courage to cut off the afflictions that make you suffer.

RECOGNIZING THE BODY

When our in-breath and out-breath become
peaceful and pleasant, our bodies begin to
benefit. In our daily lives, many of us forget
that we have a body. Our bodies often contain
stress, pain, and suffering. Often we ignore
the body until the pain gets too great. If we
breathe peacefully, this peace will be transmitted to the body. Sitting and breathing mindfully, we bring the mind back to the body and
begin to recognize its presence and release
the tension held there.

SITTING IS A PRACTICE AND A LUXURY

Sitting is a practice. The kind of sitting we're used to doing is sitting in order to work at our computers, to be in meetings, or to space out in front of a screen. So we have to practice sitting just to be with ourselves without distractions. In our time, in our civilization, sitting and doing nothing is considered either to be a luxury or a waste of time. But sitting can produce the most nourishing calm and joy and we can all afford some time to sit. How wonderful to sit and do nothing.

WHAT IS ESSENTIAL

What is essential is to train to sit quietly and mindfully. The more you train yourself, the more you can reach the deeper aspect of what you are thinking and feeling. You might think: "I'm bored!" "This is stupid." "I need to do something else right this minute." There may be old habits and old stories that are creating those thoughts and those feelings. What is getting in the way of your being able to experience the present moment? Keep breathing. Keep sitting. This is the practice.

A RIVER OF FEELINGS

There's a river of feeling in every one of us—
pleasant feelings, unpleasant feelings, and
neutral feelings. They come one after another
like drops of water in the river. As we sit, the
river of feelings runs through us and it's tempt-
ing to let a strong feeling pull us downstream.
Instead, we sit on the riverbank and observe
the feelings as they run through us. We can
name them. "This is a pleasant feeling." "This
is a painful feeling." We can do the same with
our mental formations, such as anger and fear.
Naming can be a first step in giving us some
distance from our feelings, so we can see that
a feeling is just a feeling and that it is impermanent. A feeling comes and eventually it goes.

WEATHERING THE STORM OF STRONG EMOTIONS

A strong emotion is like a storm and it can create a lot of damage. We need to know how to protect ourselves and create a safe environment where we can weather the storm. Keeping our body and mind safe from the storm is our practice. After each storm, we will became stronger, more solid, and less fearful of the storms.

We can learn to take care of the painful feelings and strong emotions emerging from the depth of our consciousness. We are more than our emotions. We can recognize what is there, "Breathing in, I know that this is only an emotion. It's not the whole of me. I am more than my emotions." This is a very basic insight. Emotions will manifest, stay for a while, and then leave. Why should we die because of one emotion? After a few minutes of practice, the storm will die down, and you will see how easily you have survived. You should start your practice before the storm begins or you might forget to do it, and may get carried away by the storm. This is why our daily practice is important.

BELLY BREATHING

Each time a storm comes up sit quietly and
return to your breathing and your body. Turn
your attention away from whatever it is that
you believe is the source of your suffering
and instead focus on your breathing. Mindful
breathing is your anchor in the storm. Bring
your attention away from your head and down
to your belly, so that you're no longer thinking and imagining. Just follow your breathing closely. Remind yourself, "I have passed

through many storms. Every storm has to pass; no storm stays forever. This state of mind will pass."

When we see the top of a tree being tossed about in a storm, we have the feeling that the tree may be blown down at any moment. But if we look at the trunk of the tree, we see it's very steady, and we know that the tree will stand strong. Your belly is like the trunk of the tree. Practice breathing with your mind only focused on breathing into your lower belly and just let your emotions go by.

NEUTRAL FEELINGS

When you sit and breathe with mindful awareness, you become aware of all the emotions
that have been ignored while you were busy
doing things. You become aware not just of
your sorrows and joys but also of your neutral
feelings. A neutral feeling is an awareness
that is neither pleasant nor painful, such as an
awareness of a part of your body that is not in
pain. With awareness, we can transform a neutral feeling into a pleasant feeling.

When you have a toothache, the feeling is
very unpleasant. When you don't have a toothache, you usually have a neutral feeling; you're
not aware of your non-toothache. When you
are mindful of not having a toothache, then

what was a neutral feeling becomes a feeling of peace and joy. You are so happy not to have a toothache in this moment. By transforming neutral feelings into joyful ones, we nourish our happiness.

TRANSFORMING CONSCIOUSNESS

The first aspect of sitting meditation is to stop and calm the body. This in itself can be a source of great happiness. But there is a second aspect of sitting meditation that can bring even more happiness. To look deeply is to do the work of transforming the depths of your consciousness. There are people who meditate only to forget the complications and problems of life. They are like rabbits crouching under a hedge to escape a potential hunter. When we look deeply we are able to see the source of our habits, perceptions, and attachments. Looking with compassion and without judgment, we begin to let go of these perceptions and are able to see the world and ourselves more clearly.

BRINGING OUR SITTING WITH US INTO THE WORLD

If you begin to feel the security and protection that arises naturally from sitting in meditation, you may be reluctant to leave this state. But we can't continue to sit forever. We can continue our mindful awareness in every action, in how we walk, talk, and work. In this way, we engage fully in life and are able to bring joy to our relationships and our world.

THE STARS OVERHEAD

No matter where we are, whenever we're sitting, over our heads there is a river of trillions of stars. We are sitting on a planet, a very beautiful planet, which is revolving in the Milky Way galaxy. When we sit with that awareness, we can embrace the whole world, from the past to the future. When we sit like that, our happiness is very great.

BE PRESENT WHERE YOU ARE

When we have the capacity to be peaceful and joyful as we sit, we can sit anywhere. We can sit in the airport. We can sit in the train station. We can sit on the bank of a river. We can sit in prison. If everyone in the world knew how to sit like that, this world would have more peace, joy, and happiness.

When we're sitting, we're truly there in the present moment; we have come home, we have arrived. We are present in that time and place; we're not pulled away by the past, the future, or by anger or jealousy in the present. When we sit like that, we sit as a free person.

A FLOWER BETWEEN TWO ROCKS

When you sit alone quietly, it's something beautiful, even if nobody sees it. When a little flower appears in a crack between two rocks, it's a beautiful sight. People may never see it, but that's okay.

SITTING AND MOPPING

How we sit can be applied at any moment during our daily lives. For example, when we mop the floor, we mop the floor just to mop the floor, and we enjoy mopping the floor. We are happy. The happiness and contentment we experience in sitting meditation can be brought into daily life. We can be happy mopping the floor.

RESTORING OURSELVES

In our daily lives we may get lost in our thinking, in our worries, and in our various projects.
To sit is to restore ourselves, to become fully
present and fully alive in the here and the now
Following your breathing, calming your body
and mind, you can become present easily and
quickly. It takes five or ten seconds for us to
restore ourselves fully and produce our true
presence in the here and the now. We offer
that quality of being to ourselves, to each
other, and to the world.

SPIRITUAL FOOD

Sitting isn't something we do as a duty or an obligation. Instead it can be part of our daily nourishment, like eating. Consider daily sitting meditation to be a kind of spiritual food. When we sit, we produce the energy of mindfulness and a feeling of ease that nourishes our joy. Try to practice sitting meditation regularly. Don't deprive yourself and the world of this spiritual food. When we can see that our practice is nourishment for ourselves and for the world, it brings us joy and the feeling that we're useful to life.

COUNTING THE BREATH

When we're first learning sitting meditation, it can be useful to count our breaths. Count "one" for the first in- and out-breath. Count "two" for the second, and so on. If your mind wanders and you lose count, go back to "one" and begin again. This exercise helps develop concentration. You may think counting to ten is easy, but counting to ten while breathing mindfully takes a lot of focus.

USING A CLOCK

If you have a clock that makes an audible
sound, try breathing in accordance with the
rhythm of the clock. This can help you stop
thinking and focus instead on your breathing.

A SITTING NOTEBOOK

It can be useful to keep a notebook to jot down notes while sitting or to write in after sitting. If you sit in the same place each time, you can keep the notebook there. If you sit in different places wherever or whenever you can, then keep your notebook with you in a bag or backpack. You can write down the thoughts that come to you, the insights you have. You can also draw. Writing when your mind is clear after sitting can be very satisfying. You don't need to read it right away. Perhaps leave it for a while, so you can continue to reflect without judgment.

WE ARE A STREAM

Even when you think you are sitting alone,
your ancestors are sitting with you. Your parents, grandparents, and great-grandparents,
whether you knew them or not, are there
inside of you. Acknowledge them and invite
them to breathe with you: "Dear father, these
are my lungs, and they're also your lungs. I
know that you are in every cell in my body."
Breathing in, you can say, "Mother, I invite you
to breathe in and out with me." In every cell of

your body, your ancestors are there. You can invite all your ancestors to enjoy breathing in and out with you. You are not an isolated being. You are made of ancestors. When you breathe out calmly, all your ancestors in you breathe out calmly. When they were alive, they might not have had a chance to sit mindfully and breathe peacefully. But now, in you, they have that chance. There is no separate self. We are a current. We are a stream. We are a continuation.

SITTING WITH OUR
SPIRITUAL ANCESTORS

When you sit, you are sitting with your blood
ancestors, but you are also sitting with your
spiritual ancestors as well. Your spiritual ancestors are also part of you. You can invite those
who inspire you; you can invite Moses, Jesus,
or Mohammed to breathe in with you and
enjoy breathing. They are also in every one of
our cells.

SITTING TOGETHER

Sitting alone is wonderful. Sitting with a friend makes meditation easier. There is a Vietnamese phrase that goes like this: "When you eat rice, you need to have soup." When you practice mindfulness, you have to have friends. When we sit together, we create a collective energy of mindfulness that is very powerful. When we sit with others, we profit from their quality of being and we profit from everyone's practice. We don't need to say a lot, but we become a collective organism and together we produce insight. When we sit together, each one of us contributes to the quality of the whole. This collective energy is more powerful than our individual energy. Sitting together is like allowing the water in the stream to be embraced by the ocean. When we hear the sound of the bell, everyone is breathing mindfully amd creating a collective energy of mindfulness. The collective energy is very supportive and effective in helping us gain insight and transform difficulties. As a practitioner we can benefit from that energy to help us embrace our pain and our suffering. You can say silently, "Dear brothers and sisters in the Sangha, this is my suffering. Please brothers and sisters, please help me to embrace this pain and this suffering."

A FLOCK OF BIRDS

When you practice sitting with others, you don't have to do anything at all. The basic practice is to be there, to follow your breathing, and to experience the joy of being together. Imagine a flock of birds flying in the sky. Every bird has its own position and each bird makes a contribution to the whole formation. They fly so smoothly together. Since each bird is part of this larger formation, they don't have to make a lot of effort. They benefit from the collective energy and don't need to work as hard. It's a pleasure to fly together like that in the sky. When we sit together, we are supported by each other. We each produce our true presence and offer that to each other.

HELPING EACH OTHER

When you sit with others, you are taking
care of yourself and you are taking care of
the group. If you see someone sitting solidly
and calmly, this can help you. Such a person
affects the whole environment. When I see
someone sitting like this, I want to sit like him.
I want to offer my true presence. My presence can also have a quality that can help the
community. The collective energy penetrates
everyone. Everyone offers and everyone
receives at the same time.

HELPING A FRIEND

There may be someone sitting with you who is holding a big block of fear or despair, but who isn't saying anything. She is trying to hold it as she sits. If you are sitting there, present and solid, you are already helping her. Your presence says, "Don't worry, I am here with you. I will help you to embrace and hold that fear and despair in you." Alone, it is difficult to hold a lot of pain. But with the collective energy of the group, it becomes possible.

A GARDENER RETURNING
TO THE GARDEN

When you sit, you are like a gardener going back to take care of his or her garden. All the plants and animals in the garden benefit from the gardener's return. They are so happy to have the gardener back. When you sit, you are coming back to yourself, to your body, your feelings, your emotions, and your perceptions in order to take care of them. That's good news.

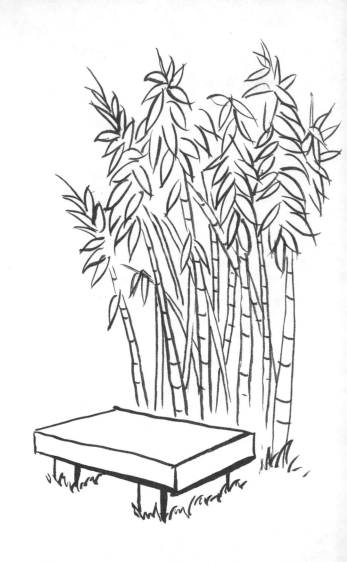

GUIDED
MEDITATIONS

Guided meditation is not a new invention.
It was used in the time of the Buddha, over
2,500 years ago. Even if you enjoy sitting in
silence, guided meditation can be beneficial.
A guided meditation is an opportunity to look
deeply into the mind, to sow wholesome
seeds there, and to strengthen and cultivate
those seeds so that they may become the
means for transforming the suffering in us. A
guided meditation can also help us come face
to face with suffering we have been avoiding.
Seeing it more clearly, we can understand its
root causes and be free of its bondage.

JOY

As you sit, you can try these meditations for bringing joy and calmness into your body. Each short verse is called a practice poem or *gatha*. The first time through, read each whole sentence to yourself. The second time through, you can just use the keywords on the third line. Silently say one word as you inhale and one word as you exhale. You can stay with those words for a few in- and out-breaths, before moving on to the next part of the exercise.

Breathing in, give complete attention to your in-breath. Wherever the breath may be in your body, feel the calm it brings. Feel how the breath cools the inner organs of the body, just like drinking cool water on a hot day. While breathing out, smile to relax all your facial muscles, and your nervous system will also relax.

These guided meditations are lights to guide us back into the present moment. They are short and can be practiced anywhere at any time: in the kitchen, on the bank of a river, in a park, whether we are walking or standing still, lying down, or sitting, even when we are working. The first meditation shows how the breath goes with the words. It works the same for all the following meditations.

1 Breathing in, I know I am
   breathing in. *(inhale)*
   Breathing out, I know I am
   breathing out. *(exhale)*
   In *(inhale)* / Out *(exhale)*

2 Breathing in, my breath grows deep.

   Breathing out, my breath goes slowly.

   Deep / Slow

3 Breathing in, I feel calm.

   Breathing out, I feel ease.

   Calm / Ease

4 Breathing in, I smile.

   Breathing out, I release.

   Smile / Release

5 Aware of my body, I breathe in.

   Relaxing my body, I breathe out.

   Aware of body / Relaxing body

6 Calming my body, I breathe in.

   Caring for my body, I breathe out.

   Calming / Caring

7   Smiling to my body, I breathe in.

Releasing the tension in my body,

I breathe out.

Smiling to body / Releasing tension

8   Breathing in, I calm my body.

Breathing out, I smile.

Calm / Smile

9   Breathing in, I dwell in the present moment.

Breathing out, I know it is a wonderful moment.

Present moment / Wonderful moment

SITTING WITH THE BUDDHA

When you sit on your own, you may like to think of the Buddha as sitting with you. You can say, "Dear Buddha, I invite you to sit with me. Please make good use of my back. My back is still good enough. And I know that when you sit, you will make my back upright and relaxed. When you breathe, I know your quality of breathing is very good. Use my lungs to breathe and my back to sit." The Buddha isn't someone outside of you. Inside each one of us there are seeds of mindfulness, peace, and enlightenment. When you sit, you give these seeds a chance to manifest. When you invite the Buddha in you to sit, he will sit beautifully right away. You don't have to do anything, just enjoy his sitting and his breathing. You can say these words to yourself as you follow your breath:

Let the Buddha breathe.
Let the Buddha sit.
I don't have to breathe.
I don't have to sit.

When you find yourself in a difficult situation or you are feeling too upset or restless to sit, ask the Buddha to do it for you. Then it becomes easy. The next exercise is:

The Buddha is breathing.
The Buddha is sitting.
I enjoy breathing.
I enjoy sitting.

The next verse is:

> Buddha is breathing.
> Buddha is sitting.
> I am breathing.
> I am sitting.

In the beginning, you and the Buddha are separate. Then you come closer. The next verse is:

> There is breathing.
> There is sitting.
> No one is breathing.
> No one is sitting.

When the Buddha breathes, the quality of breathing is light and easy. When the Buddha sits, the quality of sitting is perfect.

The Buddha doesn't exist outside of the breathing and the sitting. There is only the breathing and the sitting. There is no breather. There is no sitter. When there is a high quality of breathing or sitting, when thoughts, speech, and action are full of mindfulness and compassion, you know the Buddha is there. There is no Buddha outside of these things. I am breathing. I am sitting. There is the breathing. There is sitting. There is no one breathing. There is no one sitting.

Joy in the breathing.
Peace in the sitting.
Joy is the sitting.
Peace is the breathing.

TALKING WITH YOUR INNER CHILD

As children, we were vulnerable and dependent on others for our survival. You may have had hurts and fears as a child that were not safe to share and that you kept inside. Now, as an adult, you are no longer that vulnerable child. You can take care of yourself. You can protect yourself. But the little child in us continues to worry and to be fearful.

The child you were and the grown-up you are now are not exactly two different people and are not exactly one. The inner child is as real as the grown-up adult. They influence each other, just as a seed of corn is still real inside the cornstalk. This guided meditation is a chance to talk with your inner child, to invite him or her to come out and greet life in the present moment. We can let him or her know there is no need to worry any longer. Everything is okay now.

For this meditation, put two cushions in front of each other. Sit on one cushion and look at the other cushion and visualize yourself as a five-year-old. You can visualize yourself at a younger age if that's more helpful. Then, as you sit and breathe mindfully, you can talk to the vulnerable little child inside you. You may say something like, "My dear child, I know you are there, and I am here for you. If you have something to tell me, please say it to me."

After some moments, allow yourself to speak as that small child, expressing anything you never got a chance to share. You may complain. You may share the feeling of being fragile and helpless. Use any kind of language that feels right to you as that child. When some emotion like fear or anger comes up, that's fine.

Then, give yourself a few moments to breathe mindfully and calm your body. Speak to your inner child again, addressing the fears and anger. Let the child know you've been listening and that now you have grown up and can protect yourself so everything will be okay. In this way, you can bring your inner child and grown-up self together into the here and now and be able to more fully experience and enjoy your life as it is happening right now.

SITTING WITH DEATH

We know that life is impermanent and that sooner or later we all have to die. Sitting meditation is a wonderful way to have more awareness and acceptance of the impermanence of the body. If we can become familiar and comfortable with our fear of dying, we can begin to transform that fear. With our awareness of impermanence, we begin to live our lives more deeply, with more care and awareness. When we can envision and accept our own death, we are able to let go of many ambitions, worries, and sufferings. We are able to let go of all the things that keep us so unnecessarily busy. We can begin to live in a way that's meaningful for ourselves, for other species, and the planet.

Following our breathing, we can say:

All phenomena are impermanent.
They are subject to birth and death.
When the notions of birth and death
are removed,
this silence is called great joy.

This meditation sums up all of the Buddha's teaching. The last two lines speak of the thundering silence, which is the silencing of all speculation, philosophies, notions, and ideas.

This meditation reminds us that as long as there is the appearance of phenomena there is birth and death. When we look deeply, we see there is no birth and death. We are like the clouds in the sky, never dying, never passing from being to nonbeing. A cloud can become snow or ice or rain, but a cloud cannot become nothing. A cloud cannot die. If we overcome the notion of birth and death, we are no longer afraid of impermanence.

WRITE YOUR OWN

You can write your own practice verse to best help you produce your true presence and get in touch with your true intention. Choose one element that you want to bring into your life and one element that you want to let go. You can use this gatha in concert with your breath to return to that intention.

Breathing in, _____ (A)

Breathing out, _____ (B)

A. *[In-breath]*

B. *[Out-breath]*

Here are some examples:

Breathing in, I am aware of tension in my body.

Breathing out, I let go of the

tension in my body.

Aware of tension / Letting go of tension

Breathing in, I calm my agitation.

Breathing out, I feel at ease.

Calm / Ease

Breathing in, I'm in touch

with the cool autumn air.

Breathing out, I smile to the

cool autumn air.

Autumn air / Smiling

RELATED TITLES

Awakening Joy
by James Baraz and Shoshana Alexander

Be Free Where You Are by Thich Nhat Hanh

Being Peace by Thich Nhat Hanh

Breathe: A Journal by Thich Nhat Hanh

Breathe, You are Alive! by Thich Nhat Hanh

Calm, Ease, Smile, Breathe by Thich Nhat Hanh

Deep Relaxation by Sister Chan Khong

The Energy of Prayer by Thich Nhat Hanh

Happiness by Thich Nhat Hanh

Making Space by Thich Nhat Hanh

Mindful Movements by Thich Nhat Hanh

Moments of Mindfulness by Thich Nhat Hanh

Peace of Mind by Thich Nhat Hanh

Monastics and visitors practice the art of mindful living in the tradition of Thich Nhat Hanh at our ten mindfulness practice centers around the world. For a full listing of practice centers, or for information about retreats, visit plumvillage.org or contact:

Plum Village
33580 Dieulivol, France
plumvillage.org

Deer Park Monastery
Escondido, CA 92026, USA
deerparkmonastery.org

Magnolia Grove Monastery
Batesville, MS 38606, USA
magnoliagrovemonastery.org

Blue Cliff Monastery
Pine Bush, NY 12566, USA
bluecliffmonastery.org

European Institute of
Applied Buddhism
D-51545 Waldbröl, Germany
eiab.eu

Thailand Plum Village
Nakhon Ratchasima,
30130 Thailand
phfhk.org

The Mindfulness Bell, a journal of the art of mindful living in the tradition of Thich Nhat Hanh, is published three times a year by our community. To subscribe or to see the worldwide directory of Sanghas, or local mindfulness groups, visit mindfulnessbell.org.

The Thich Nhat Hanh Foundation supports Thich Nhat Hanh's peace work and mindfulness teachings around the world. For more information on how you can help or on how to nourish your mindfulness practice, visit the foundation at tnhf.org.

PARALLAX PRESS

Parallax Press is a nonprofit publisher, founded and inspired by Zen Master Thich Nhat Hanh. We publish books on mindfulness in daily life and are committed to making these teachings accessible to everyone and preserving them for future generations. We do this work to alleviate suffering and contribute to a more just and joyful world.

For a copy of the catalog, please contact:

Parallax Press
P.O. Box 7355
Berkeley, CA 94707
Tel: (510) 525-0101
www.parallax.org